HUSBAND

FATHER

FAILURE

Poems

HUSBAND FATHER FAILURE

Poems

KG Newman

The Nasiona
San Francisco

HUSBAND FATHER FAILURE: Poems

Copyright © KG Newman, 2019

Published by *The Nasiona*

All rights reserved. No reproduction, copy, or transmission, in whole or in part, may be made without written permission.

For information contact :

nasiona.mail@gmail.com

https://thenasiona.com/

Author photograph by Justin Rampy.

ISBN: 978-1-950124-07-7

Contents

THE GIFT

PREMATURE 3

THE LAST BORN IN VOLATILITY 4

THE AFTER LOVE 5

FLAWED SUPERHERO 7

BOTTOMLESS DROPPING ROCKS 8

EPIGENETICS 10

BEFORE THE K AGE 11

FATHERHOOD THERAPY 12

MY DAUGHTER'S BALANCE 13

MY SON'S LIONS 14

THE CREDULITY

IMPENDING DIVORSE 17

BOX SCORE 18

MORNING ROUTINE 19

PAST DUE 20

SMOKE SCREEN 21

THE SEPARATION 22

EXPLANATION FOR PORCH CANDLES 23

THUMB WAR 24

THE DECEMBER DRAGONFLY 25

BRIEF HISTORY OF BROKENNESS 26

WITHIN BOWED WALLS 27

SASTRUGI IN EARLY SEPTEMBER 28

KENSHŌ 29

THE WAR

FINDING THE LIMEN 33

SURFACE FIRE 34

THE SURVIVAL SLANT 35

MY SON FORGETS WHY WE DIVORCED SO I TELL HIM 36

VALENTINE'S DAY 38

THE CRITICAL ANGLE 39

FIG LEAVES 40

HIGH LEVERAGE SITUATION 41

INEVITABLE 42

THE SETTLING

THE SUNDIAL 47

BURIED DECREE 48

ABSOLUTE MAGNITUDE 49

THE ROOT FEAR 50

OUR CHILDREN'S VIEWING ROOM 51

ALMANAC FOR MY FATHERHOOD 52

BULLSEYE 53

REVELATIONS DOWN THE DISTRIBUTARY 54

CONSEQUENCES OF DETACHMENT 55

THE AWAKENING

AT THE BREWERY DOWN THE STREET 59

LAVISH SADNESS 60

POST LIMERANCE 61

THE KING OF PERHAPS 62

HOW WE UNDERSTAND THE MEN WE'VE BEEN AND ARE 63

THE BEER GENE 64

KINTSUGI 65

LOVE ABOVE REPLACEMENT 66

A CREEPING HEADACHE 67

TENNIS BALL, WINDSHIELD 68

ABANDONED 69

HISTORY OF TRUTHS 70

THE ACCEPTANCE

AM PROMMESTRIA 73

THE CURVE OF UNDERSTANDING 74

DRIVE TIME DREAMING 75

WEED & BINKIES 76

THE WASPS' PENDING EXTINCTION 77

THE VIBRATIONS OF WIND AND WINGS 78

CALLOUSING 79

GETAWAY CAR 80

AMERICAN REFUGEES 81

THE PLEA

GASLIGHTING YOURSELF 85

TERMINAL LOVE 87

PERDITION IN C MINOR 88

CREVASSES 89

RECKONING 90

MEANWHILE, ANTS 91

NEW MORNING CLOTHES 92

POLYDIPSA 93

ACKNOWLEDGMENTS 95

ABOUT THE AUTHOR 97

*You open your windows to good air
blowing in from who knows where,
which you gulp and deeply inhale
as if you have a death sentence. You have.
All your life, it seems, you've been appealing it.
Night sweats and useless stratagem. Reprieves.*

                 — Stephen Dunn, "Before the Sky Darkens," 2000

THE GIFT

fear,
hope;

holding love together —

THE GIFT

PREMATURE

Like any good father, I pull my son from
the river, drag him by his arms up
the embankment, his Lilliputian shoes
cutting tracks through mud that rapids
rush to erase. Because the city beyond
these mountains is no longer as we

envisioned it. Because the derailed train
is now a skein of lichen on a slick boulder
that was my gut when we heard
he wasn't okay, and I couldn't say a word.

I sit beside him as he coughs up water. I ask
who I am but get no reply — instead overhead
hawks are heard but unseen and he
remains so still he could be anyone's son,

found the way cairns steer us up
the face as early summer mornings
preheat to a promise the mountain
isn't sure it can fulfill.

THE LAST BORN IN VOLATILITY

I cut my knuckle
disassembling his crib
and sadness rushed me
and all my indecisions,
this being the last
of the baby stuff
stacking up in the garage.

Days later, wife's question
still unanswered, I wandered
her garden for a poultice
of comfrey. Our son
helped me. The sun hung
like the crooked, fast clock
in our kitchen.

When we were finished
I wrapped my finger
and tucked him in bed,
stuffed paws standing guard
against loud memories and
along one rail, covering
a nail slightly jutted out.

THE AFTER LOVE

Once we stuck
each other with
every sharp barb
we could think of
there was calm
about the kitchen,
no more clinking
dishes or traps
snapping underneath
the sink.

Once, we fought
the idea of
our love as
an artifact,
stray sleeping dogs
of lonely America
matted and
snoozing happily
on suburban curbs
across the states.

Now we know
we are a poem
written on a
hotel notepad;
we are what's left
of our son's
bradycardic response,

reconciliation attempts
in the light of
the shallow end
of the pool.

FLAWED SUPERHERO

The morning Stan Lee died I put my son in his Spiderman shirt
for day care, wondering when he'd comprehend
each late-night kitchen argument or the fears and burdens
attached to the most unexpected blessings.

Afterward, on my ride to work, I imagined grayed Parker
attempting to convince embittered Mary Jane
that he never thinks of Gwen Stacy or the Black Cat
and all those crises of confidence are well behind him now.

Even so, a known lie is sometimes met with hope.
That morning, from my son — *It's just a mask, Dad* —
up all night listening, agreeing to have Parker's confidence
anyways, as if he'd just been bit, strong today,
making dad promise the same.

BOTTOMLESS DROPPING ROCKS

Jax hands me rocks and tells me it's ice cream.

This, after long coming to the understanding
I'm insatiable.

Nowadays I add up all my things
and they add up wrong,
even if my greatest weakness did lead
to my greatest reward: Rock ice cream,
breaking my teeth as I try to chew through
to sweetness.

*

I never say thanks
you never say sorry

while Little People figurines
listen to us argue

from their bus in
the picture-filled family room

as the TV buffer, long
worn thin, ruins

little bud's nap with sirens.
So we take him outside:

He picks up rocks,
watches them drop.

They rain on his shoes,
yours and mine, painlessly —

I find myself smiling at you,
you might back soon too.

EPIGENETICS

Because he's two and can't, I tee up
the ball, déjà vuing to the worn net
in my father's basement. When he demands
I don't adjust his hands, he knows better.
He's always known better but is just now
figuring out ways to say so. As though
he's already grown, swinging through
the bunt sign, as though it's really possible
to inherit muscle memory.

BEFORE THE K AGE

Father pioneered analytics in Netscape forums
and this was debate time.
Mother drank. I Nintendo'd intently
with a game full of little hopes.
Mornings came. My eyes grew heavy
customizing the barrel speeds
of synthetic kings of swing.

There was a red dress
in the extra bedroom
spinning from the fan,
but who put it there?
Mother's tumblers made water rings.
They were semi-opaque,
like the state of my brain just then.

The homers I hit sounded like guns.
"Data over beliefs," he always repeated.
In my game full of little hopes,
conflict raged: Needles and lies
giving rise to an ugly kind of strikeout age,
with my humidor heart splintering at its stump.

FATHERHOOD THERAPY

Before he fell asleep in my arms
by the campfire again
he saw something in the flames.
First a cat, then a monster,
then a burning tree, the same he
climbed earlier in the afternoon,
high enough to look out
at Pikes Peak and see the snow
still holding strong in late June,
his dad down below with
a blanket tied around the neck
as a cheap superhero.
After I tuck him in the tent
I toss another log on and start
to see things too. My father.
His father. My son as a father,
embers of generations
specked into the wind; men
staring long enough
to remember who they are.

MY DAUGHTER'S BALANCE

My daughter's walking a rope she strung
from the porch post to the tree.
In three months she'll be in fourth grade —
five years since we all bowled
on our first date — and she's picturing
how insignificant the traffic accidents
are from above, her concentration in full force
amid the hundred-story wind.

Through kitchen windows, in front of a cracked
backsplash, we rehash old fights a hundred
new ways: Metered sacrifice with a side effect
of resentment, mentioned alongside
the warning label — *Loving blended family.
Serious leadership issues.*

But we always have her courage as our equalizer:
Eventually, amid our hundredth dispute
over laundry, our daughter takes her baby brother
back out front, strings up the rope,
and waits.

MY SON'S LIONS

He keeps them on a shelf as long and slender
as a clocktower hand —
the minute, not the hour —
all stuffed, plastic and reglued ceramic sorts
that'll soon be binders of baseball cards
of the early '90s variety, hoarding Ken Griffey Juniors
as I did my father's George Bretts.
I normally dealt them in my most authentic Majestics,
on suburb blocks far and wide.
What a great trade, my father used to say to introduce
long-lasting summer evenings, watching the game
and hoping the housing market didn't collapse.

THE CREDULITY

*denial,
avoidance;*

some blind faith —

IMPENDING DIVORCE

In a precisely lighted kitchen,
I hear my wife in code:
Says the spokes are broken.
Says please contribute, not robotically.

It's that time of night:
We're listening for de-icing trucks.
If salt noise were a traceable scent,
it'd go on for miles,

but the bypass won't reopen anytime soon.
Its frontage roads have snow and trash
stacked even higher. I've reported
on a few trend stories in my time, and
the words of this particular enterprise
are so desperate they misspell themselves
in an effort to miss print. It's against
my ethics to reveal my sources,

even in an effort to reverse this course.
Too many corn grains have been fermented.
Two, off balance. Two whiskeys
for fiction, or the arsenic for truth.

BOX SCORE

My son, running in a clearing between three peaks,
comes to an abandoned diamond amid the thistles.
It was baseless, but that's okay — he didn't know
the difference. To start he picked up a busted ball
and tossed it in the air, to no cloud in particular.
Soon he was imitating his grandfather's swing.
He played the way his father finally did
after wasting all the at-bats that counted.
He planted what was left of his small bag of seeds.
All around him trees waited to be made into bats.
His arm went numb. He pitched until he was
no longer pitching, but was himself the glove
receiving every heater on the freezing spring day
he was made from, having reached the end
of what the game could reasonably explain.

MORNING ROUTINE

Things are going well in the public relations campaign
in my mind

even though
problems hang over the trees of just-waking suburban streets
shortly before I graduate my first divorce

in three years yet at the bottom of my class,
cracked diploma with
my name likely misspelled —

if I knew what to do
I'd yell it out
in the shower —

but for now,
to the porch,
where it is becoming sunny
there is weed
and I can eat
your plums
you left
in the icebox.

Inspired by William Carlos Williams' "This Is Just To Say"

PAST DUE

The whole day was like
decelerating through
a yellow light.
Somebody let
all the horses out
from the fairgrounds.
Driving around them,
by the open space,
I thought I saw a turkey
mangled
in the barbed wire fence
but passing by
it was just
a tattered black trash bag.
All the clarity made
for hypocrites' kryptonite:
Setting up for an ending
where we forgive each other
for everything
before lightning
sets the porch on fire.

SMOKE SCREEN

At Green Heart
all the budtenders are women.
I buy an eighth and go to
Altitude, where they are women too,
tatted but lacking grunge — they vape,
hit the gym between shifts.

When couples counseling is suggested
I suggest the young blonde
who says she's a fair arbitrator
and she'll hear me out.
The waterfall and Incense makes
it all sound and smell so promising.

I open with a long list of vices
by which we barely coexist.
Just tell me your best possible outcome
with this, she says, setting a pinner
on the end table. I reach for my lighter
in the hopes I can remember.

THE SEPARATION

Life is a metaphor for the errant grill cover in my backyard
and chocolate chips melting in my hands, the feeling
of not standing you before but now I walk around
shouting your name in the best way.

Every time I put the cover back on the grill, the wind
rips it off. Then the dog marks it up. I'm tempted
to give him a bowl of chocolate chips just so
he'll lie down quiet and not mess things up for one minute,
like when our son's asleep and he barks out your name
as if he's got nothing better to say.

EXPLANATION FOR PORCH CANDLES

Since the goal was to make it to death together,
I wanted our home to have an open concept —
conglomeration wallpaper filled with city skylines,
the Space Needle seamlessly beside the Eiffel Tower
and outside, fences built just to clarify the prairie
as grain sorted itself inside the tower and traffic
couldn't be recollected. It was all necessary for birds
to remember their migration routes and for our couch
to not pull us too deep, hugs rusted shut and fingers
the tangled bones we wanted not a day too soon.

THUMB WAR

I want the digit pain again
and sore wrist with it.
The shut lips of my father
and our quality time
as we played at the kitchen table.

His calloused, vitiligoid hand
pinning me down,
then gifting space to escape.
The shouting from the neighbors
making us somber for a moment.

There's little more to remember.
The storm door still broken,
and from my frayed upstairs landing,
listening above the wall's half-handrail,
paint-stripped and splintered.

THE DECEMBER DRAGONFLY

who frequents my snowy winter acre,
petrified bees and butterflies in his stomach,
who quaffs alone in the blackened bird pond:

I would've never known him only I quit
on kitchen fights for sunset beer dinners and
a cold throat when I smoke so that's when

I caught him at work deep in the yard,
buzzing around the weeds as if searching
for his ancestor's two-foot fossilized wing.

BRIEF HISTORY OF BROKENNESS

The year I was born
a historic hailstorm came.
Everyone lost cars, windows.
The shards never fully swept.

In time, the suburb recovered.
Insurance copped for solar panels,
HOAs bought replacement birds.
I grew up assured of the sun

even though my closet overflowed
with raincoats. I had two Nintendos.
We weren't rich in other ways
despite a chandelier on the porch.

Here I struggle today, still timid
under clouds, but relentless.
Carefully releasing everyone I love
into the dry, bright sky.

WITHIN BOWED WALLS

All I asked for was a reasonable word.
Finally I hit her with the worst ones
I knew: I. Don't. Care. Maybe it was true

or maybe since the dragonflies escaped
the seams between the laminate
floor beams have widened — perhaps

because I didn't let the "wood" adjust
enough before installation — and in turn
that's created a curse worse than

we ever could've imagined, riches and
children and an additional cabin and
for what? There's no sense in a discussion

if we can't stand on even ground
in our kitchen, where three years prior
we tore out the uneven backsplash,

cementing our own with haste
while laughing at the raw incompetence
of the former owners.

SASTRUGI IN EARLY SEPTEMBER

In the summer underlain
the evergreens sung with birds
even if the boots we wore
signaled our time was short.
At least I thought it was.
Later, grayer, I'll say
we should've had a third.
But now all that mattered
was keeping the kids warm,
by hike or at ballgames
flaked in white, to where
we'd out-weathered
climate change so as to
adapt to what we really are.
Husband and wife,
or father and mother.
Whatever makes snow
in the summer fun, and
keeps summer summer,
even as buntings freeze
and drop from the trees.

KENSHŌ

Everything on the front lawn,
there were decisions galore
amid the dust and dirt
of the much-needed garage cleanup.

The donate pile had to grow,
although I procrastinated greatly
by piling all bud's baby stuff
high in the garret.

With a black bandana snug under
my eyes like an avoidant bandit,
I took the broom to each corner
to stall further, sweeping out leaves

living there since he was an infant.
In the end I ended up keeping
the bouncy seat and the mutual
resentment with his mother:

There was nowhere to put that —
too wide for the crawl space
and too used for second-hand —
but on the way back from Goodwill

I saw a pride of excavators
flattening dirt in another new development
and more in-progress buildings
just down the street from the house.

It reaffirmed my belief in belief
and the prosperity to be had here.
But what still wasn't clear was how
to re-arrange the garage to achieve

our desired Wu or if I could actually
eventually use each axe
and half-bent rake without the urge
to make a bonfire of it all.

THE WAR

*anger,
vindictiveness;*

the biggest mistake —

FINDING THE LIMEN

Divorce coming like a war I can't afford,
bud and I ride our bike down
to the reservoir. Somewhere during therapy
he falls asleep in his seat behind me,
and his Hulk slips from his grasp:

When he wakes we take frantic laps
around the water, searching for his figurine.
Empty, I return by myself in the following days
after leaves fall and snow comes and goes,
eyes straining from studying fringes of the path
with small hopes of returning home a hero.

It's harder to grip the meaning of the loss
than the loss itself — that's filled by
an Amazon order set to arrive at our door
any day now, even while each spring morning
I kiss my wife's cheek as she turns away in bed,
still awaiting word on the park ranger's search.

SURFACE FIRE

I woke alone, covered in yellowed newspaper,
not the substantive sections but rather
the ad inserts — and through
the cracked window wafted the smell
of a wild fire.
I never got you that trench coat
now in five different colors across my face
or any of the sentimental gifts either,
like horseback riding lessons that
always advertised toward the back
of the Sunday section,
by which time I'd be high and you'd be done
with coffee and on to vodka.

THE SURVIVAL SLANT

How do we live in deceit?
We tear the truth and
weave it into a lie —
spiders on a signal line —
waiting for change
to make itself known.
When it doesn't come
we need serotonin fanged
directly into our brains,
seizures to restore order,

and what's left to cling to
is the disagreement itself:
third child or not,
Denver or Indiana,
a dinner of black-tie variety

standing at the end of this.
No whiskey/martini overpriced.
You'll give back the ring.
We'll both say what we mean
and it still won't mean a thing.

MY SON FORGETS WHY WE DIVORCED SO I TELL HIM

alternate endings to keep his respect.
It was something we ate. We left one morning
and forgot where our room was.

I fell off a ladder just so
at the exact moment of our dog's heart attack.
She drank all the light and became translucent.
We got bent up in a pistachio picker.

It was like a C-grade horror flick
watching what we'd grown
shake free from the trees, the machine vibrating
to keep us from getting up.

We never cleaned the grisly wreckage,
and soon we became a side show
to the world's largest pistachio
with packed minivans racing down the highway
so families could glimpse the mangled couple
and teach their kids an example.

The pumpkin patches nearby were unable
to keep up, even with Jason-laden corn mazes.
People came and placed bets on what
exactly happened, some guessing
the number of infidelities.

I still can't go to that farm.
I remember her white, with purple all over.
The machine's repository filled with

nothing but blanks. Her dying
in front of everyone else as she left
no breaths for me.

VALENTINE'S DAY

The constant threat to take
the kids out of state, coupled
with seasonal affective disorder
and my job moving from downtown
to an industrial district —

                                    right off
I-70 next to the old Colonial Motel
where hazmat crews in white suits
removed mold from what was once,
in each room, a love for
at least something —

                            has me hitting
the hash pen hard shortly before,
with anger and one hundred dollars,
I buy her a sweet card, flowers.

THE CRITICAL ANGLE

Driving, the look on her face
isn't love; isn't anger;
neither a desire
to change the station
nor turn it down.
It's more like surrender
through which
her old shoes
seem brand new
and a sharp intelligence
reflects off
her necklace,
the festoon of diamonds
knowing exactly where
to direct the light.

FIG LEAVES

On the last sips of summer
we all had ballgames to attend
what with the divorce rate
and herpes percentages
never anyone reading
the fine print
the neighbors were drunks
a haboob was brewing
sand grits already lined
our spit as technicolor trees,
unsure of the season,
tried to be everything
to everyone.

HIGH LEVERAGE SITUATION

Patrick asks how the offseason is going and I reply
that I'm Bryan Shaw, beleaguered reliever,
we in separate vectors but still the same in essence:
Rich baseball men on the brink.
His pregame Call of Duty is my marijuana.
His flabby athlete body is this reporter's emotional detachment.
Even the blown leads, harder to compare, still do:
torpedoed dates or kitchen shouting waking up wonderful kids
on a perfectly decent Friday night after covering a game.
So there's much at stake this upcoming summer.
I need calls on the black. The time to prove
this narrative's worth. I need the need
to re-find the power position and
a consistent landing spot. Confidence.
Reverse projected WAR, hope in the dirt and ink.

INEVITABLE

The sophistry is at an all-time high
and there's rivers all over the room.

She yells and tells me I'm selfish
as if it's an order. I remember her

as someone who sent a fruit basket
to a co-worker's ill grandmother

yet she must verify our love
via Instagram. She thought her boxer

was tough even after he pissed
on the floor during a break-in.

She's on the poster for reverse
evolution, on alert at all times

for a woolly mammoth siege.
I'd believe it was love if not

for the shiv hidden just outside
the cave. Now she's raving about

another phantom infidelity and what
can I do but smoke and put everything

that's ever been us — the rings,
this sting, the little bud — into a canoe

and attempt to stay afloat through
these rivers all over the room.

THE SETTLING

*destruction,
detachment;*

casualties of love —

THE SUNDIAL

I needed the time to direct me the way I wanted.

I thought of no clocks. In every aspect of design,
as I stabbed the paper plate, as I guessed north,
as I poured gray paint into a gray rock,
I envisioned life for them like toxophilite warriors
unburdened from sacrificing a best buffalo's sinew.

To be strong in this is after one night, our family,
my perilous reward, will wake to sun dogs,
where there is no estimation, and come to form
a warmth igniting deadwoods which are wounds,
reconciling the duff, and accepting my quiet.

BURIED DECREE

The kitchen table has grown
so dense with yellowed
newspaper and unpaid bills
that plates have no space,
dinners standing by the sink.
Yet even in this neglect, pens
know signatures, dishes steam
under hot water, the way we
throw ourselves into things,
eating without tasting,
growing clutter that distracts.

ABSOLUTE MAGNITUDE

All this time pretending to love
could have been spent
learning astrophysics or
studying Voltaire.

Instead the dogpiles
of pre-depression childhood
are the only flint left
in the woods I find myself in,

and I strike them together
hoping not for warmth
but to burn the whole forest
in the pattern of a diamond.

THE ROOT FEAR

The doc on the post office gets serious
when the talk turns to shipping babies
in the early days, when regulations
were vague and — I'm surmising —
it was an option at mediation.

My second-worst fear is this PBS special ends
and we're only further
from a middle again.
I'll remain stone. You'll threaten —

our son could become
an untrackable package
on the wagon trail forth,
and not back, between
Philadelphia and New York.

OUR CHILDREN'S VIEWING ROOM

Switzerland banned lobsters from being boiled alive
the same day she finally followed through, and signed
the papers. But I still wondered how the Swiss
replaced one murder for another, or if they now gave
the lobster's family forewarning, or at least
a viewing room. Can an old love, disrupted by
taste buds, learn new tricks? I don't know.
This isn't about love. This is about lobsters,
how they shriek in the boiling water as if
already understanding the feeling of being eaten.

ALMANAC FOR MY FATHERHOOD

In my dreams, wheat fields. I search them alone, in a tux. This dirt, white as snow. My father is afraid of cold. All I remember is what I remember most — phlegm in his throat, red encroaching from the corners of his eyes. My father, he fears failure and losing hair. *Your mother and I kept it together as long as we could,* he tells me. The dirt is indented from plights before mine. I start to run to find those souls that have found the meaning of themselves, but find only a lone silo. My father, he fears clouds, the way they can take any shape or the blurred scene where I come to be. It's an unseemly truth that surviving in the corn requires one to abandon all sense of direction.

BULLSEYE

I am not a scarecrow
stuffed with the organs of farmhands
and endangered birds,
a loose knot at the end of the rope
in the distant bell tower.
They screwed me twice
by lawsuits and Twitter mob.
Their megaphoned insults
hacked into my dreams.
Reputation dies hard is what
the next generation
said to my son
as they profiled my footprint
via iWatch hologram on the handball
wall of the playground.

REVELATIONS DOWN THE DISTRIBUTARY

My son, for example, arrived midstream,
proof of everything even though the river
didn't provide a mirror.

Sprung up, seeing us grow deep
in wheat fields as old-time ballplayers,
vintage mitts catching flies off the bounce.

Will come out with it: Questions over hefeweizens,
explaining what happened with his mother,
focused as we were, drunk, at the river.

CONSEQUENCES OF DETACHMENT

Dinos didn't read
and now they're extinct.

Imagining myself as
the Bachelor, stoned
the entire show.

The inability to speak,
text or even email
has a tendency to
build upon itself:

soon among beautiful women
I'll forget what T-Rex stands for
or how to process
the extinction of myself.

THE AWAKENING

*ragged,
healing;*

searching for self —

AT THE BREWERY DOWN THE STREET

I moved past yelling at clouds and began emailing
vile sentiments to every advertising executive I could,
explaining how their vapid spots are the reason
I'll never buy their products again.
All believed me except the beer companies.

Those suits rebuffed my dispute that a man and a woman
smiling and clinking pilsners on the patio were something closer
to kitsch than non-fiction. If bitterness reflects
a false sense of depth — an inability to see beyond hops —

then a six-pack should get you over it quickly, they said.
At that point it was hard to argue much more, over a pilsner,
while observing truth at the brewery down the street. Woman
in a red dress, with a well-dressed man. Dark mash thrashing.

LAVISH SADNESS

What's the point of an entry rug
so fancy I can't wipe my feet?

And if the speed of light can be slowed
to 38 miles per hour by ultra cold gas,
is there any realistic chance
I'll ever escape this?

Life's questions pass themselves around,
answers somewhere between
the biometrics of her tongue and
the Giethoorn of my dreams —
before the scene where Nabokov
nearly invented the smiley —

where I am the mopey monarch
in need of a cat piano, demanding
my fleet of gondolas fan out and
bring me every feline immediately,

to be categorized by tone and, after
the music, converted into Tabriz.

POST LIMERENCE

Everything beautiful soured.
Bagged and set on the curb.
Bodies inverted. Coins sliding
out from the deepest recesses
of our pockets before word came

about crayoned clouds we thought
we could pop. Their rain might
open up what we tried to erase.
Feeling in our faces. Cycling
through time's greenbelts, apiaries.

Even with no sun days flashed by.
Our sheets filled like lungs.
This was our accord:
Wounded inside a Nickelodeon-lit
playroom, we grew.

THE KING OF PERHAPS

Standing in my yellowed, weed-ridden grass,
the gnats ate away, no one to blame but
my legs. Of all the things I could control,
the lawn wasn't one — I was the king
of just enough, of should be happy, of perhaps.
The Roundup label said death.
This time its warning booklet only
gave me bad ideas. My favorite squirrel
dead from yesterday's poison, there
at the base of the tree. How many of us
could stand such chaos right outside
their suburban door, with more
traffic than normal for a quiet Sunday
and somewhere in between
I tried to smile; I waxed my truck;
across the street neighbors yelled
enough for everyone, a cadence of curses
drowned out only by sprinklers, working
for once, a wet ratchet in my mind.

HOW WE UNDERSTAND THE MEN WE'VE BEEN AND ARE

Opening Day loomed and the bullpen
was still in question.
                        I could save games
but I could not, with one arm,
also set them up.
                My father tried
to do that in the early 90s and ended
with two blown shoulders,
withered ligaments at his feet.
                            He needed
to take more blame for wayward outings,
the messy divorce and the cutters
he said would be here, and went there.
                                I need
the Hoyt Wilhelm experience —
after my own war I volunteer to fight
I return, kiss my son, don't say much,
knuckleballing my way to the majors
at 29 and recruiting my father to catch
a pitch so good he couldn't.

THE BEER GENE

Imagining the liquor store
my grandfather used to frequent:
Was he known by name and if so
did he feel guilty about how often
he clanged the front bell —
back for just beer, not hard stuff,
his way of justifying the buy?

Now imagining the brewery
my father made his favorite —
he definitely met my stepmom
there — and where won't my son
be able to visit a dispense?
The opportunities for intoxication
are endless even if staggered
by generation, bedridden old men
hanging on just long enough
for their son to light their joint.

KINTSUGI

The timing of my addiction
came like the first generation
to know about global warming
and final to choose to do
nothing about it.

Thus it's become a comedy where
the lungs are afraid to laugh.
Flaccid high-fives, all downhill
on bikes: Summer's cooling wind
now winter's sobering weapon...

But December forecasts warm enough for
my grandfather's reconstructed clay pipe
to keep paying homage with smoke holograms
across the sky as I ride: Truth in the distance,
thinned hawks perched on certain roofs.

LOVE ABOVE REPLACEMENT

I exterminated colonies in dugouts
at my father's unmown field.
I blasted the nests with my bat
and paralyzed the wasps with
a flurry of his third base signs.

This was before lit empty ballparks
had auras other than the aura
of my father. It was pre-sabermetrics
or sportswriters' emphasis on
Three True Outcomes.

In those innings, well before wind
stopped carrying my pop-ups
beyond the wall, I longed for freedom
to swing 3-0. With split adjustments,
I always knew what was coming —
at least that's what I believed,
and following games, helping
my father rake the dirt, I'd long
for an honest conversation
about my mother or why
the best batter's eyes
are wide, and dark.

A CREEPING HEADACHE

Where do I go when
the motive becomes elusive?
When the umpires consult
the commish mid-game
and even midnight
Law & Order reruns
become unable to sedate?

My idea is to eat
the freshest fruit first,
even if that means wasting
last week's avocados.
The idea is, admittedly,
more of a pipe dream:
Each desire becoming
more diluted than the next,
happiness mixed with
hands that always
reek of gasoline.

TENNIS BALL, WINDSHIELD

For a decade I tried to think of what to say.
How often you'd run off, tires squeaking
as you leaned and shouted *This is how
I'll take your kids.* How many bathtub wicks
you lit trying to understand love and

I can tell by your eyes you've seen, but
may not recognize, it again. How would
you describe the experience of hatred
and passion and fear that keeps me adjacent
to you? I hoped to be the husband you
wanted to build, the reason you dreamt
about the new backsplash in the kitchen,

and I'll still steam your coffee and repair
the mailbox post, massage your scalp
in warm water. We have become a sum
of lesser love: a prison of sun: I'll set
rat traps and take our garage back,
toss all the junk, sweep and shove
boxes aside so that you can pull
into your stall with ease.

ABANDONED

This is the winter when
the snow doesn't stay long
on our skin and our hope
is in the slim apertures
of the fir leaves where
sunlight slots through to moss.

Blame me if I don't remember
every closed ski resort
where we learned love:
Empty chairs and untouched runs
still accessible by snowshoe

but your view?
Rusted lift stumps,
the rotted warming shack.
Not enough snow this season
and, in still-unexplored bowls,
the likely risk of landmine
which I am just fine
with negotiating.

HISTORY OF TRUTHS

There was once a coastal backwater
where this Kansas cow pasture is today

is the first stanza of Saturday's musing
at the packed nature and science museum.

It's startling how even in the crowd
a quiet infiltrates the ears to turn

my baobab upside down, which is
actually right side up. It's in this state —

with monkey bread severed from
millennial branches and the K-T boundaries

of my life in exhibits all around (i.e., pipe
tomahawk rusted with resin and blood) —

that the fantasy of jackalopes truly
hits home, like the closed door of finally

knowing whether we're alone
in this universe or not — it's part

euphoria, a little uneasiness, but mostly
a wistfulness for this place to be a sea again.

THE ACCEPTANCE

scarred,
walled-off;

what's done is done —

AM PROMNESTRIA

Like many I quit on love young —
always falling out harder than in —
and now I stay waiting for
a Madame von Meck of some sort
to pen offers of friendship and
finance for all future composing.
I know it's far-fetched — like
feelings of peace as I leaf through
adagio sonatas of old — for
to accomplish such a feat
of epistolary adoration requires
a match maker of the ancient
variety, an art form of complex
emotions, long before the public
classical station exploited
stories of Tchaikovsky's patron
as a guise for a fund drive.

THE CURVE OF UNDERSTANDING

As a kid I'd ride my bike
around a dirt path circling
the old munitions factory
with boarded-up windows
and columbines cropping up
just outside the building's
outstretched shadows.
This was before I deemed
revenge a viable source of
renewable energy I could
pedal a lifetime on and
after I gave up depending
on what I'm feeling at the
moment. I hope there's no
retribution from the senate
of chipped red bricks
for all the misconceptions
and times I snipped fence
to crawl onto the grounds,
looking for another wall
to tag, not with red or blue
but with hieroglyphics
and simple sketches
of what the place
looked like in its heyday.

DRIVE TIME DREAMING

When I fall in love with the local DJ
because her voice is so damn confident as
she rattles off hip hop facts each morning,

I know it's probably time to trade in
the old pickup for a new, souped-up
midlife crisis with XM radio. That way

the only DJs I'll be listening to are
the syndicated brain-melters, and there's
no chance of bumping into them

at a remote, say Dunkin' Donuts, say
it's 4/20 and my opening line is,
"I've got us the perfect strain of weed."

WEED & BINKIES

Four in the morning.
Little bud across the hall
is shouting *DA-DA* from his crib,
static on the Vivaldi
in my nearly snuffed dream where
a hall of doors
open and shut in unison.
The subtitles are Arabic,
the connection hot-wired
from my neighbor's apartment.
Behind my couch the line grows
through the wall to watch
the training video, a collection
of scruffy-necked slims
who believe fatherhood,
with its weed & binkies,
is something
that can be taught.

THE WASP'S PENDING EXTINCTION

Nostalgia gave way to worry when the wasps on our porch
disappeared overnight. Why they fled was obvious —
our toxic love and the umbrella nest left behind
begging the question of what could have been —

like if we had set out colored paper instead
of letting the deadwood pile like a fire hazard
on the side of the house while the wasps convened

assemblies on how to reinvent themselves,
arthropods siphoning arthropods
having now been taken by us.

THE VIBRATIONS OF WIND AND WINGS

In the buzzing blue box
strapped to my back,
there's our last honeybees.

If you need a queen, I have that,
if you need a queen to kill that queen,
I have that too.

I have in my jacket
out-of-print trail maps
outlining every overgrown egress.

I can improvise nutrition
from a scrapped comb
and white pine bark;

with patience from a whipped line,
the settled past's hooked mouth
tugs toward the surface.

I hold memories of you in the antigens.
I carry your hairbrush to better
understand your thoughts.

The stings don't slow me down:
I am thickened. This pride
that once distanced you

packs up light as twine.

CALLOUSING

Young, I searched for you to not only tie my shoes,
but also to make sure the tongue
was perfectly straight.

Later, after breaking up with every princess
on the playground, I switched
to elastic laces and found recess
is best enjoyed with the freedom to dash

between playing kickball and house —
a basic understanding of the paradox of love
and desire —

for older now, running with stiffer yet similar form
as my second grade self,
my adult polyester laces keep coming undone.
There's strength in symmetry

but the knots are consistently askew. And the more
I sweat, the further I get,
what's left to do is turn up the rap,
take off my shoes.

GETAWAY CAR

Ferociously swinging and missing at flies
reminds me there are no mistakes
in life, only fateful accidents,
and that these flies were likely
once an errant brush stroke as
Bob Ross painted me in my kitchen.

So I've decided to embrace stepping out
from how everything's been framed —
perpetually angry wife beside
thirsty lilacs potted on the table —

just to recall how the radio sounds
ad-free in the middle of the night,
no difference between now and then,
every note dope, that strong, chin music.

AMERICAN REFUGEES

At the foreign arboretum
we zigzag among species
which may or may not
be poisonous to our love
as trip hop plays
from heavy stratus clouds.

Now is what we've been
putting off —
figuring things out,
evaluating how many pines
to sacrifice to rebuild
our house again.

At any minute, the children
will bore of the silo.
And soon, with robe and gavel
from three-story trees,
they'll oversee this litigation,
wondering whose job it is
to rotate the fields.

THE PLEA

guilty,
remorseful;

clutching my son —

GASLIGHTING YOURSELF

First, out of love for my son,
and also out of conflicting loyalties
between fatherhood and freedom,
I looked in the mirror and repeated
I could live both a full and broken life.
If I couldn't be every wife's
standard, certainly I could be some,
say devoted dad one minute, an amalgam
of reliable and impulsive the next.

The issue was addiction
had no season, was as nagging
when she redefined nag as when
something greater than love
rose toward the sun on a park swing.
Just yesterday at the stadium
I'd seen the groundskeeper
roll out new sod for the upcoming season,
and I imagined what they did with
the old grass, chunked in spots
where outfielders dove for balls
they may or may not have caught.

That's how I walked the empty concourse,
two clenched fists, wishing for a third.
And when I exited the gates,
the fate of the team seemed
beyond sabermetrics, beyond
a strong bullpen and the most professional
of approaches to each at-bat.

Sometimes on late-night Twitter,
trolls would point all that out. Sometimes,
they'd just let this fool's faith ride.
Sometimes there were just enough
characters to declare what I wanted —
a winning team, one I'd take my son
to see, gruff major leaguers packing dips
and sliding headfirst into home.

TERMINAL LOVE

When I adjust to grief
I see inside my skull,
the asbestos and offal,
the trees outside
turning to skeletons
amid rushed comparisons.

Maybe grief isn't what
I thought it was as
stones fill flower beds
while a red horizon indicates
poor air quality today —
and it's not just today

I'll be coughing for.
The X-ray dye will show
something spectacular.
The doctors will laugh.
I won't be able to stop
smelling her hair.

PERDITION IN C MINOR

Drunk, I left myself for dead
down in the ravine
where ironweed stood firm
amid butterfly carcasses.
After the wolves came,
a silence: crushing,
wider than the prairie
where singular cattlemen
rocked and puffed
their pipes and beyond
the manure composts
a garbage man walked,
covered in grime,
dragging a corn stalk.

CREVASSES

Sometimes we have to accept the truth
as a little less plain:
                       Polar bear boars —
weak from a shortened peak seal season
in which whatever one wanted (blubber,
love, money) rose from the ocean —
still traverse, undaunted, for food across
historically thin ice.
                    Never mind they
are absent dads — I practice this speech
ten times in the mirror for the kids,
hoping an uplifting animal intro takes
the sting out of the word *divorce*
and when I finally admit it's not right
to blame others, or climate change,
for pain radiated from frazil stabs
upon our plunge into the Arctic.

RECKONING

The history of forgiveness that is
your sonhood, and the little
that is not, will be heaped
together in a thick deposition,
expensive defense of fitness,
the hugs and the drugs
depicted on tussocky ground
beside sun-rusted flatirons.

The cabin I cannot complete
without his help, the momentum
of two different Disston saws:
Firs shedding in September to pack
the land a couple inches toward
winter, insulating itself until
spring, waiting for wood to be
carved back to bone.

MEANWHILE, ANTS

I dream of hearing her hair curling
from the shower that's never warm.

My head must be buzzed,
the hair picked up with cut hands.

And outside, the grass is sacrificed
for a fire pit for rings:

the very patch I'd worked
so hard seeding that spring. Meanwhile,

ants keep stampeding from
the porch screen to the kitchen,

circling around the family Maltese
as she dies. Soon I'll ask

the only question left:
What is readiness?

A red dress with long curls
falling down an open back.

NEW MORNING CLOTHES

And people fell in love and into careers,
abusive relationships and dead-end jobs,
money, gangs, fame, obscurity.
They fell into pools, drunk, and off bridges,
into each other on trains and then to a mass
of feet to pick up their papers, all scattered about
the one time they need to be on time.
Some fell into themselves — strange selves,
abyss selves — a fall that disappears
a penny. Some fell into suburbs
they couldn't find with a map,
and then fell into them again,
years later, by only the stars.
People fell into comas and out of habits,
by what they held and what slipped away.
There was never any stabilization to be had —
even if one fell with the wish of never
rising back — because what can be said
about the futile battle with gravity, a sublet
of fate:
        What cliff, I don't remember.
On the way to another falling out and
I noticed you, across the notch:
Snow, your new morning clothes.

POLYDIPSIA

Drinking my beer while holding
my baby is the closest I come
to being Buddha — night after
night, neighborhoods of my liver
dying off while he outgrows
one onesie, then the next.
It's like scoops of flickering
streetlight plus the gravel
we rode in on, all the fine bits
of rock and time I can fit
in a fist. It's cross-eyed looks
we give each other at
the end of every sixer,
birds in blue who flock
to smoke, grass growing
in the patchy backyard where,
in the corner, I pour out
the last sips and hope
to grow a tree.

ACKNOWLEDGMENTS

Premature appeared in The Literary Nest ….. *Epigenetics* appeared in Dime Show Review ….. *My Son's Lions* appeared in Former People Journal ….. *Impending Divorce* appeared in Verse Virtual ….. *Morning Routine* appeared in Ithaca Lit ….. *Smoke Screen, Survival Slant, Inevitable, Bullseye* and *Terminal Love* appeared in The Bitchin' Kitsch ….. *The Separation, The King of Perhaps* and *History of Truths* appeared in Triggerfish Critical Review ….. *Explanation for Porch Candles* appeared in Penultimate Peanut ….. *Within Bowed Walls* appeared in Glassworks Magazine ….. *Sastrugi In Early September* appeared in Visitant Lit ….. *Finding The Limen* appeared in White Wall Review ….. *My Son Forgets Why We Divorced So I Tell Him* appeared in Constellations Journal ….. *Our Children's Viewing Room* appeared in Two Hawks Quarterly ….. *Almanac For My Fatherhood* appeared in Rocky Mountain Revival ….. *Consequences of Detachment* appeared in Word Fountain ….. *The Beer Gene* appeared in Progenitor Literary Magazine ….. *AM Promnestria* appeared in Rat's Ass Review ….. *Weed & Binkies* appeared in Queens University Literary Magazine ….. *Gaslighting Yourself* appeared in Grey Sparrow Journal ….. *Perdition In C Minor* appeared in The Lark ….. *Reckoning* appeared in Mush/Mum ….. *New Morning Clothes* appeared in Crack The Spine ….. *Polydipsia* appeared in The Quotable ….. *Brief History of Brokenness* appeared in Digging Press ….. *The Last Born In Volatility* appeared in The Finger Literary Journal ….. *Flawed Superhero* appeared in Pennsylvania English ….. *Box Score* appeared in 2 Bridges Review ….. *Before The K Age* appeared in Funicular Magazine ….. *Thumb War* appeared in Thirty West Publishing ….. *Absolute Magnitude* and *Meanwhile, Ants* appeared in Straylight Literary Magazine ….. *Fatherhood Therapy* appeared in Thin Air Magazine …. *At The Brewery Down The Street* appeared in The Blue Nib …. *American Refugees* appeared in Goat's Milk Magazine …. *My Daughter's Balance* appeared in Lou Lit Review.

ABOUT THE AUTHOR

KG Newman is a fourth-generation Coloradan and sportswriter at *The Denver Post*. He lives in Castle Rock with his wife and two kids, and believes there's a bit of honesty in everybody — it just takes the right woman, daughter, son, or Sunday doubleheader at Coors Field in order to bring it out. In addition to hiking, camping, skiing, cycling, and living out a lost dream in men's summer league baseball, he's quick to shoot in pickup hoops and always swings the driver way too hard on the back nine. The 2012 valedictorian of Arizona State's Walter Cronkite School of Journalism, his first two collections of poems, *While Dreaming of Diamonds in Wintertime* and *Selfish Never Get Their Own*, can be purchased on Amazon. For more info, poems and contact information, visit kgnewman.com.

www.ingramcontent.com/pod-product-compliance
Lightning Source LLC
Chambersburg PA
CBHW020946090426
42736CB00010B/1281